RESOLVED

13 Resolutions for LIFE

STUDENT EDITION

New York Times Bestselling Author

ORRIN WOODWARD

WITH ROB BROWN

OBSTACLES
PRESS

RESOLVED

13 Resolutions for LIFE

STUDENT EDITION

ORRIN WOODWARD
WITH ROB BROWN

First Edition, August 2015
10 9 8 7 6 5 4 3 2

Published by:

Obstaclés Press
200 Commonwealth Court
Cary, NC 27511

orrinwoodward.com

ISBN: 978-0-9964612-3-8

Cover design and layout by
Norm Williams, nwa-inc.com

Printed in the United States of America

To those who RESOLVE to change the world
through changing themselves.

Contents

Contents

Introduction

In 2011, when I wrote *RESOLVED: 13 Resolutions for LIFE*, I did so to share the resolutions that had so radically changed my own life. The results of this labor of love have been nothing short of mind-blowing. For within the first year, the book was named an All-Time Top 100 Leadership Book and became the framework for the bestselling Mental Fitness Challenge Program.

Still, when Principal Rob Brown of American Leadership Academy in Gilbert, Arizona, contacted me to discuss using the resolutions in *RESOLVED* to create an entire K–12 school curriculum, I was a little surprised. Principal Brown had written to me:

> I am the principal at American Leadership Academy in Gilbert, Arizona, a K–6 elementary charter school. As the name implies, we are patriotic, leadership-driven, and focused on academics. It's the leadership part that drew me to this school. I love that we teach children the principles of leadership. When I was introduced to *RESOLVED*, I was amazed at how simple and powerful each chapter was. I said, "What would happen if we taught this to kids!?!"

What would happen, in his and my opinion, is the students would accomplish private victories, which would lead to public victories and then leadership victories, finally resulting in a legacy to pass on to the world. After Principal Brown, Chris Brady (CEO of LIFE Leadership), and I discussed the idea further, we realized that beyond a school curriculum, *RESOLVED Student Edition* is just the first of many books in a series that will eventually become the Children's Leadership Library.

Rob Brown is not your average principal. The hunger to learn and the passion to teach are evident in everything he does. Indeed, the book you hold in your hands would not have been completed if not for his drive to finish what he starts. Furthermore, I cannot think of a better person to partner with in spreading the power of resolutions to transform lives than a principal on the educational front lines. It has been a pleasure working with Principal Brown.

Finally, the principles taught in *RESOLVED* can now help anyone at any age. Each section concludes with a workshop. That's where the real power lies. Complete each workshop as you read. As you apply these principles, you will gain confidence in making choices. You will really begin to understand the importance of the choices you make and how they will influence your life.

I have taught for years that vision is tomorrow's reality expressed as an idea today. It's time to stop talking about education transformation and start living it. This book has turned the dream into reality.

Sincerely,
Orrin Woodward

CHAPTER 1

PURPOSE
Resolved: To Discover
My Purpose

*I know that finding my purpose is key to my
happiness and effectiveness.*

At 5'10" and 175 pounds, John Wooden did not have the body of a typical basketball player. Yet he became one of the greatest college players and head coaches in college basketball history.

As a player for Purdue, he led his team to victory at the 1932 Helms Foundation unofficial national championship and was admitted into Purdue's Hall of Fame. His coach described him as the best-conditioned athlete that he had ever coached in any sport. How was this possible? At almost half the size of a basketball player by today's standards

(Shaquille O'Neal is 7'1" and 325 pounds), being a successful basketball player would surely seem impossible. But what Wooden did not have in size he made up for in quickness, speed, and determination. He used these skills to turn the impossible into the possible.

After college, he coached high school for eleven years before moving on to the NCAA, where he became the head coach for Indiana State and later UCLA. He led Indiana State to the NAIB finals and UCLA to a legendary ten NCAA championship titles in twelve years. What most people know about John Wooden is that he was one of the greatest and most respected coaches. What most don't know is that he had many more challenges to overcome on the path toward becoming a champion than just his height.

When Wooden began coaching for UCLA in 1948, they told him that he would be coaching his team in a state-of-the-art facility. But it was almost seventeen years before UCLA built a new facility. In the meantime, Wooden's teams were forced to practice in less than pleasant conditions. They met for every practice at the old Men's Gymnasium, where they shared the third floor with the wrestling and gymnastic teams. Wooden and the players joked that the gym was the B.O. Barn because it was stuffy and dusty and smelled like awful body odor. It would take his team sixteen years of hard work in the B.O. Barn to win their first NCAA title in 1964.

> **"If you don't have time to do it right, when will you have time to do it over?"**
> **—John Wooden**

Wooden had a long list of excuses he *could* have used to explain why UCLA should never have been a great basketball team. He used none. Instead, he was committed to his purpose of helping others achieve their own greatness (what he loved most about basketball). He said that it was what happened in practices that gave him joy and satisfaction.

More than winning games or championships, Wooden was passionate about teaching others how to reach their highest potential. It did not matter to him that the team was not winning championships. What made his players champions was that they strived to reach their full potential, lived their purpose every single day, committed to a superior work ethic, and would take no shortcuts along the way. To Wooden, the numbers on the scoreboard were not as important as the process used to achieve them. He knew his players were already win-

ners because they put forth their best effort and remained focused on their purpose to be the best players they could be. He said:

> There is a standard higher than merely winning the race: Effort is the ultimate measure of your success....When it's over, I want your heads up. And there's only one way your heads can be up—that's to give it your best out there, everything you have.... When you give your total effort—everything you have—the score can never make you a loser.

Dave Meyers, former NBA player and captain of one of Wooden's championship teams, once shared:

> As a pro...absolutely nothing else mattered but winning. If you missed a shot or made a mistake, you were made to feel so terrible about it because all eyes were on the scoreboard....Coach Wooden didn't talk about winning—never. His message was to give the game the best you've got. "That's the goal," he would tell us. "Do that and you are a success. If enough of you do it, our team will be a success." He teaches this, he believes it, and he taught me to believe it.

There are two scoreboards in life: an inner scoreboard (what you know to be true about yourself, your character, integrity, work ethic, and effort) and an outer scoreboard (how others see you, the number of things you have achieved). Wooden created a championship team by choosing to focus only on his purpose and his team's inner scoreboard.

> "Talent is God-given; be humble. Fame is man-given; be thankful. Conceit is self-given; be careful."
> —John Wooden

You too can choose which scoreboard to use in life. By choosing your inner scoreboard, you understand that with effort, determination, and commitment to your purpose, sooner or later you *will* meet your goal, just like Wooden and his amazing championship teams did.

WORKSHOP CHALLENGE

Talk About It

1. What challenges did John Wooden face on his path toward becoming a champion?

_____

_____

_____

_____

_____

2. How would you describe Wooden's attitude when he faced these challenges?

_____

_____

_____

_____

_____

3. What was Wooden's purpose?

_____

_____

_____

_____

_____

4. What was more important to Wooden than winning? Why was winning not important to him?

_____

_____

_____

_____

_____

_____

5. What can be tracked on your inner scoreboard? Outer scoreboard?

_____

_____

_____

_____

_____

6. How will focusing on your inner scoreboard affect your outer scoreboard?

_____

_____

_____

_____

_____

Go and Do

1. MAKE A LIST. John Wooden was passionate about basketball. He used this to develop his purpose and help his players become the best they could be. Think about the things you are most passionate about or very good at. Write them down.

_____

_____

_____

_____

_____

_____

_____

2. CREATE! Start creating your inner scoreboard by writing down answers to the following questions: Who am I? What do I love to do? Who do I do it for? What do they want or need? How do they change as a result of what I give them?

_____

_____

_____

_____

_____

_____

_____

3. HELP SOMEONE. Make a plan to use your talents
    to help others. What would you like to do? How will
    you do it? When will you do it? Record your plan
    below.

    _____

    _____

    _____

    _____

    _____

    _____

    _____

    _____

4. After you have completed your plan, record the
    results below.

    _____

    _____

    _____

    _____

    _____

    _____

    _____

    _____

CHAPTER 2

CHARACTER
Resolved: To Choose
Character over Reputation

*I know that my character is who I am, and my
reputation is only what others say that I am.*

There was a man named Ludwig von Mises. He lived in Austria and was famous in his country as an economist. That means he understood how government, businesses, and people worked together for the good or bad of their communities and country. Ludwig was fifty-eight years old when the Germans started World War II. He fought with all his might for his country not to allow Hitler and his government into his homeland. He warned that the country could not survive. His country didn't listen.

Many people threatened his life. They told him that if he didn't change what he said, they would kill him. He bravely refused. He knew what was right, and he wouldn't choose wrong simply because someone threatened him. In fact, he and his wife had to sneak out of their country and flee to America to find safety. He spent the rest of his life teaching others the value of freedom.

> "Economically considered, war and revolution are always bad business."
> —Ludwig von Mises

We learn some really neat things from Dr. Mises. Perhaps the most important have nothing to do with economics. He showed us through his example that he had integrity. Integrity means that we never choose to do wrong on purpose. There are three simple ways that we can demonstrate integrity: never lie, never cheat, and never steal. Of course there are more, but choosing integrity shows that we respect ourselves and others.

Ludwig also showed us that character means we should do what's right. While integrity is choosing not to do wrong, character is choosing to do right even if it's difficult. It takes serious courage to do what's right. For example, John, an older boy, bullied little Billy at school. Tom watched it all happen but didn't participate. Tom showed integrity by not joining in bullying Billy, but he did not show character. For Tom to have character, he must have the courage to do what's right; he must have the courage to defend little Billy from being bullied.

For us to have character, we must know what we believe in. One of the great problems with people all over the world today is that most don't know what they believe in. We can't know right and wrong if we don't have a firm foundation of belief. Choosing to have character and integrity means learning what is right and what is wrong and choosing to have the courage to make the right choices no matter what.

Dr. Mises had courage. Courage doesn't mean we can't feel nervous or scared. It means we believe in something so much that even if we feel scared, we are willing do it because it is the right thing to do.

> "Only the individual thinks. Only the individual reasons. Only the individual acts."
> —Ludwig von Mises

Let's choose to have character. Let's choose to have integrity and courage regardless of what others do or say around us. If we do, we will find peace and an increased ability to lead ourselves and others in the right directions.

WORKSHOP CHALLENGE

Talk About It

1. What is character?

_____

_____

_____

_____

2. What is integrity?

_____

_____

_____

_____

_____

3. What is courage?

_____

_____

_____

_____

_____

_____

4. How did Ludwig von Mises show character, integrity, and courage?

_____

_____

_____

_____

_____

5. When have you seen someone show character, integrity, or courage? What happened as a result?

_____

_____

_____

_____

_____

Go and Do

1. MAKE A LIST. How can you develop character, integrity, and courage? Write a sentence committing yourself to become a person of character, integrity, and courage.

_____

_____

_____

_____

2. CREATE! What is one thing that you can do each day to show character, integrity, and courage? Try doing it every day for a week, and record what happens.

_____

_____

_____

_____

_____

3. HELP SOMEONE. Teach a friend or family member what you have learned. Tell him or her what you are doing. Record your experience.

_____

_____

_____

_____

4. One of the best ways to help others is through example. After your week, see if anyone noticed what you did, and record the experience.

_____

_____

_____

_____

_____

CHAPTER 3

ATTITUDE
Resolved: To Have a Positive Attitude in All Situations

I know that by listening to my positive voice and turning down my negative voice, I will own a positive attitude.

As far back as the time of ancient Greece, which had a culture based on the idea of intellectual, moral, and physical perfection (an idea the ancient Greeks called *paideia*), people started forming the concept of a "perfect mile," the fastest a human being can possibly run that distance. For a very long time, it was held that the perfect mile was exactly four minutes, and people dreamed of meeting that perfect time and even beating it. Until 1954, however, no man or woman had ever run that perfect mile. Enter Roger Bannister, a medical student who believed that, through the proper use of science and training, he could break the four-minute barrier.

Inside every person's head are two voices. One is our positive voice. It sees the good in every situation. The other voice is our negative voice. It sees the bad in everything. We can't eliminate either voice entirely, but we can learn to turn one up and the other down. Happy people learn how to turn down their negative voice and turn up their positive voice, leading to a positive attitude and outlook on life. The difference between positive people and negative people is as simple as the choices they make about which voice they will listen to.

Roger practiced running constantly, everywhere, pushing his body harder and harder. This exercise reduced his heart rate to only fifty-four beats per minute. This allowed his body to maintain a larger oxygen reserve and made breaking the four-minute mile physically possible.

He tried and failed many times to conquer that four-minute mark. Many people criticized him for even trying, and some made fun of him for believing he could do what they believed to be impossible.

> **"The man who can drive himself further once the effort gets painful is the man who will win."**
> **—Sir Roger Bannister**

Roger turned up the positive voice in his head and turned down the negative voice. He knew that those negative thoughts were like weeds. If he let them grow, they would ruin what he had worked so hard for and felt to be true. So when he recognized a negative thought, he got rid of it. He pulled it out and threw it away. His attitude remained positive and drove him to keep trying.

Roger worked hard at keeping a positive attitude. There are always distractions that seem to be important in the moment, but keeping a positive attitude about achieving our long-term goals helps us focus on what is most important.

In 1954, on a chilly day in Oxford, England, Roger sought to reach and even alter the idea of the perfect mile by running a mile in under four minutes. He and the other runners were to race on a wet cinder track in a biting, cold wind. At six o'clock in the evening, the runners were at the starting line. Roger and two team-mates made a plan to help him break the record. His friends would run fast in front of him to help cut the wind, preserve his energy, and keep him moving fast enough to have a chance to break the record.

The one-mile race required them to run four laps around the track. The first lap was run at a fast 57.5 seconds, and they covered the first three laps in 3:00.7 minutes. That meant he would have to cover the last lap in just under one minute. He was already tired, but he lengthened his stride and gave it everything he had. He collapsed, exhausted, at the finish line. He had done it! Roger Bannister ran the mile in 3:59.4, the first person to do so in recorded history! He ran (and even beat) the "perfect mile"!

In the next five years, hundreds of sub–four-minute miles were run. Why? **Attitude!** Roger had shown that it was possible, and now every-one's attitude had changed. They had turned up that positive voice, which made it possible.

One last important attribute of attitude is to have a thankful spirit.

When we choose to have a thankful spirit, we choose our positive voice, and we can overcome challenges on life's journey. The voice that a person chooses to listen to determines the outcomes of the races in his or her life. Choose wisely. Attitude is everything.

> "Doctors and scientists said that breaking the four-minute mile was impossible, that one would die in the attempt. Thus, when I got up from the track after collapsing at the finish line, I figured I was dead."
> —Sir Roger Bannister

WORKSHOP CHALLENGE

Talk About It

1. What are the two voices in your head? Can you identify experiences in your life when you heard one or the other?

   _____

   _____

   _____

   _____

   _____

2. What are some dangers of listening to your negative voice?

_____

_____

_____

_____

_____

_____

3. How do you feel when you listen to your positive voice?

_____

_____

_____

_____

_____

_____

4. How did Roger Bannister deal with his negative voice?

_____

_____

_____

_____

_____

_____

5. What lessons can you learn from Roger about how to handle your negative voice?

_____

_____

_____

_____

_____

_____

6. What difference would it make if you listened to just your positive voice and turned down your negative voice?

_____

_____

_____

_____

_____

_____

Go and Do

1. MAKE A LIST. Start noticing your two voices. Fill in the chart. Make a tally mark for every time you notice one of your voices for the next twenty-four hours. See which one you hear more. Which one did you listen to more? What did you learn?

Positive	Negative

---

2. CREATE! Develop your own method for turning up your positive voice and turning down your negative voice. Keep track of your progress as you did in Step 1. Write about at least one experience daily where you chose your positive voice and the difference it made. In one week, start the process again, and see how you have already changed.

---

3. HELP SOMEONE. Can you help others by listening to your positive voice? Share with a family member or friend what you are doing, and teach him or her how to do it. Invite this person to join you in the process and to discuss each other's progress every week. Be sure to record everything. Remember, keeping a record will not only help you stay on track, but it will also be the inspiration for new ideas in the future.

_____

_____

_____

_____

_____

_____

_____

_____

_____

CHAPTER 4

VISION
Resolved: To Have a Clear Vision of What I Want to Become in the Future and Then to Plan for It

I know that the more clearly I develop my vision, the more I am able to make it happen.

On the surface, Willard Carroll Smith Jr. was just an ordinary boy. He came from an ordinary family, lived in an ordinary town, and went to an ordinary school. You might think Smith would have grown up to be just another ordinary man, living an ordinary life, working an ordinary job. But inside this boy was something extraordinary, something so extraordinary that he would be able to catapult himself to superstardom by the time he was sixteen.

What this ordinary boy, whom we now know as Will Smith, had was a dream (a vision) and a plan for achiev-

> **"I wake up every day full of hope, positive that every day is going to be better than yesterday."**
> **—Will Smith**

ing that dream. This all started when he was a teenager and his girlfriend broke up with him. His feelings were crushed. Even so, he knew he had a choice to make: he could pity himself, or he could pick himself up and move forward. "In my mind," Smith said, "I wasn't good enough." Then he pushed that thought aside and said, "I remember making the decision that I will never not be good enough again." After that day, Smith set a goal and implemented a plan to achieve fame, fortune, and excellence.

At sixteen years old, Smith and his friend DJ Jazzy Jeff released their first album, which went on to earn them the first Grammy Award for a hip-hop act. The fame and money started rolling in. However, Smith had no financial experience, and it was not long before he'd spent nearly all of his money. Smith was devastated and embarrassed. He was now faced with another choice: abandon what he envisioned he could become and go back to living an ordinary life or continue on with his plan.

He chose to pursue his vision and used his fame from winning the Grammy to turn his rap act into the sitcom *The Fresh Prince of Bel-Air.* The show became a huge success. When it was over, Smith envisioned entering the highly competitive movie industry. He decided his next goal would be to become "the biggest movie star in the world." The only problem was that no moviemakers wanted him in their movies. Again, Smith was faced

> **"Don't compare yourself to others. That's when you start to lose confidence in yourself."**
> **—Will Smith**

with a choice: give up on his vision or keep striving for it. Smith chose to never give up. Five years later, he landed his first opportunity, which led to his appearing in many successful movies, including *Men in Black*, *The Pursuit of Happyness*, *Wild Wild West*, and *Shark Tale*.

A once ordinary boy became an award-winning, multimillionaire superstar. Many people would say he was just lucky. He would tell you differently. "Just decide, and the universe will get out of your way," he said. "You're in a universe that says two plus two equals four; two plus two is going to be what I want it to be."

Smith had the vision of what he wanted to be, and he was determined to achieve it. He took charge of his thoughts and his actions. Nothing would get in his way that he could not choose to overcome. His inner voice told him to always believe in his vision and never give up.

> **"Being realistic is the most commonly traveled road to mediocrity."**
> **—Will Smith**

Rejection and failure might come, but they would only fuel his commitment to achieving what he envisioned he could become. "If it was something that I really committed myself to, I don't think there's anything that could stop me from becoming president of the United States," Smith declared.

WORKSHOP CHALLENGE

Talk About It

1. What was so extraordinary about Will Smith?

   _____

   _____

   _____

2. How do you think he felt each time he was faced
   with a new challenge?

   _____

   _____

   _____

   _____

3. How did he overcome the challenges he faced?

   _____

   _____

   _____

   _____

   _____

4. Will Smith had a plan. Why do you think this was important?

_____

_____

_____

_____

_____

5. What lessons can be learned from hearing Will Smith's story?

_____

_____

_____

_____

_____

_____

Go and Do

1. MAKE A LIST. Write down your vision statement of what you want to become in the future. Post the statement somewhere you can see and review it every day.

_____

_____

_____

_____

2. CREATE! Imagine yourself ten years from now. Keeping your vision statement in mind, write a story about what your life will be like. What will you be doing? Where will you be? What will you have accomplished? Who will be in your life?

_____

_____

_____

_____

_____

_____

3. HELP SOMEONE. Read Will Smith's success story to a friend. Share your own vision statement. Talk to your friend about the importance of having a vision for the future and setting goals to achieve that vision. Ask your friend what he or she would do if something got in the way of achieving his or her vision. Share what you would do.

_____

_____

_____

_____

_____

_____

_____

CHAPTER 5

PLAN AND DO
Resolved: To Make a Game Plan for My Life

I know that a failure to plan is a plan for failure.

Have you heard of Lou Holtz? He is recognized as one of the greatest college football coaches of all time. He is short and skinny and has a lisp. He was born to a poor family and grew up with low self-esteem. His parents divorced when he was just a kid. He even said, "When I was growing up, we needed a raise to be considered poor."

So how does a kid from such an unlikely background grow up to be one of the greatest college football coaches ever? Let's see if we can figure it out.

Lou's dad quit school when he was in third grade. No one in his family had ever gone to college. So when his high school coach came to his house to tell his parents that Lou should go to college,

> "Ability is what you're capable of doing. Motivation determines what you do. Attitude determines how well you do it."
> —Lou Holtz

they didn't know how to respond. They didn't have the money, and Lou hadn't even been that great a student in high school. His mom loved the idea though, and she took a second job at night so that he could go to college. Her sacrifice ignited a fire in Lou, and he was determined to never let her down.

He began by setting goals. At one point, he wrote out 108 goals! But what he did next set him apart. He wrote out a plan to accomplish each one of those goals, and then he pursued his plan. He worked hard and kept track of how he did.

Lou had to adjust his plans sometimes, but he always kept working toward his goals. He took responsibility for his choices and never blamed anyone else if he failed. He credits this as his formula for success. This is how he succeeded and how we can too. The steps are simple. We call them PDCA: Plan, Do, Check, Adjust.

> "If you're bored with life, if you don't get up every morning with a burning desire to do things, you don't have enough goals."
> —Lou Holtz

First, we must identify our goals. They can be as small or as grand as we want to make them, but then we must PDCA.

What is a *plan*, and how does it help us? A plan helps us identify the steps we will take to achieve a goal. The plan gives us a direction, a path to start on, and a road to achievement. Asking good questions about our plan will help us know if it is going to help us reach our goal.

The best plans in the world are worthless unless we act on them. The second step, then, is to *do* the plan. As

Nike says, "Just do it!" We might be a smashing success, or we might fail, but unless we *do*, we will never know what works and what doesn't. Doing allows us to test our plan and to see if it actually works.

The third step is *checking* to see if our plan is working. If we are on the right track, we can continue to do, but if we notice that some changes need to be made to the plan, this is where adjustment comes in. *Adjusting* is simple. It is adding to, taking away, or changing steps in our plan so that we can reach our goal.

It is important to keep track of our goals and PDCA along the way. This helps us remember our successes as well as our mess-ups and helps us make the right adjustments along the way. Some goals can be reached in a few days, while others might take years or even decades to achieve. It doesn't matter. If we write our goals and PDCA, we will figure out a way to accomplish whatever we dream.

So dream big! Make it fun. Make it a game with yourself, and win every time! But remember that even an occasional failure is a win if you make the proper adjustments.

WORKSHOP CHALLENGE

Talk About It

1. What was so amazing about Lou Holtz?

_____

_____

_____

_____

_____

2. What was the secret to his success as a coach?

_____

_____

_____

_____

_____

3. What have you learned about goals?

_____

_____

_____

_____

_____

4. What is PDCA?

_____

_____

_____

_____

_____

5. What difference would it make if you practiced setting goals and doing the PDCA process?

_____

_____

_____

_____

_____

_____

Go and Do

1. MAKE A LIST. Make a list of goals. Include one goal you would like to accomplish now, one goal you would like to accomplish in a month, and one goal you would like to accomplish in a year.

_____

_____

_____

_____

2. CREATE! Write a plan for accomplishing each goal. Start doing your plan. Check it and adjust as needed. Keep track of your progress every week.

_____

_____

_____

_____

_____

3. HELP SOMEONE. Choose someone to teach this to. Share what you are doing, and ask this person to help you be successful. Then invite him or her to do the same. Write about your experience.

_____

_____

_____

_____

_____

_____

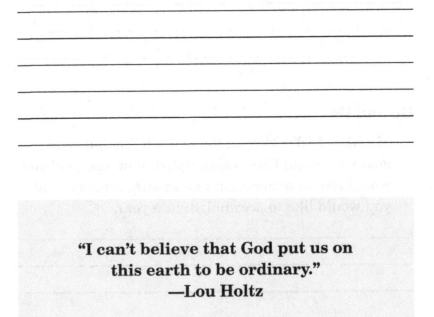

"I can't believe that God put us on this earth to be ordinary."
—Lou Holtz

CHAPTER 6

SCOREBOARD
Resolved: To Keep Score in the Game of Life

*I know that the scoreboard forces me to check
results and make needed adjustments
in order to win.*

In the 1960s, computers were becoming the wave of the future. Up until then, businesses tracked all of their inventory and sales by hand using pen and paper. Store owners, managers, and accountants painstakingly recorded, line by line and column by column, what was being sold, what was purchased, how much each item was purchased for, and the profits and losses. This process of "keeping score" was slow and tedious.

About this same time, a businessman by the name of Sam Walton was managing a small chain of discount stores in Arkansas. Just like other business owners, he too was keeping score of everything by hand. Walton's goal was to grow his business by opening stores nationwide. He knew that in order to do this, he would have to start doing some things differently and would have to learn to keep score of his business in a new way. He was not exactly sure what that would look like, but he knew computers had the potential to help. So in 1966, Walton enrolled in an IBM school for store owners where he could learn how to use computers to improve the operations of his business.

> **"Outstanding leaders go out of their way to boost the self-esteem of their personnel. If people believe in themselves, it's amazing what they can accomplish."**
> —Sam Walton

Through what he had learned at the IBM school, Walton was able to create a new method (scoreboard) for tracking his business using computers. The new scoreboard allowed him to collect more information, or data, on what was working in his stores and what needed to be improved. He and all his employees, not just managers, could track their store's profits, purchases, and sales. They could even see which stores were doing better than others (the winners and losers). The scoreboard helped hold managers and associates accountable for their store's results while also giving them the freedom to offer suggestions for improvement and the ability to learn from other successful stores.

As Walton and his employees studied the data every week, using the new information to improve each store, the business continued to grow. What Walton liked most about using the scoreboard was that the data did not lie. The scoreboard showed him the truth about how his stores and employees were performing.

Walton discovered that he could turn using the scoreboard into a game to incentivize his employees. First he would define the game, or set the goal. Then he would educate the team on the goal, explain how it would be accomplished, and set them loose to play the game. Along the way, they would track the game using their scoreboard. When the game was over, everyone came together to check and

> **"Commitment is the key to success to everything."**
> **—Sam Walton**

study the score. Based on the score, local managers would be held accountable for either winning or losing the game, and adjustments for improvement would be made. During one game, Walton promised to wear a grass skirt and dance the hula on Wall Street if his company could achieve a goal of 8 percent pretax profits. The game and the potential reward of seeing their conservative boss dance the hula on Wall Street energized the entire team. They met their goal, and Walton followed through on his promise. "It was one of the few times one of our company stunts really embarrassed me," he said.

Today, Sam Walton's business (Wal-Mart Stores, Inc.) is over 4,000 stores strong. We now know them as Walmart. There is probably one in your own town! Every store continues to keep score by collecting data and sharing it with all the employees. They continue to study which stores are performing well and which ones are not. The scoreboard gives a clear picture of their successes and failures. It is undeniable that the scoreboard has helped make Walmart the successful, billion-dollar business it is today. It has helped everyone there face the reality of their failures as well as spread their successes across the entire company.

WORKSHOP CHALLENGE

Talk About It

1. What does it mean to "keep score"?

_____

_____

_____

_____

_____

2. How did Sam Walton use his scoreboard?

_____

_____

_____

_____

_____

3. How did using a scoreboard improve Walton's company?

_____

_____

_____

_____

_____

4. What information did Walton's scoreboard reveal?

_____

_____

_____

_____

_____

5. What should be done after studying the score?

_____

_____

_____

_____

6. How can a scoreboard be used in other ways or areas?

_____

_____

_____

_____

_____

Go and Do

1. MAKE A LIST. Using a scoreboard can help you track your progress toward personal improvement and meeting goals. How can you use a scoreboard to help you with the goals you have made? Make

a list of things in your life you could track using a scoreboard.

_____

_____

_____

_____

2. CREATE! Choose one goal, and build a scoreboard. Write your goal at the top. Then make a list of actions you will need to take to accomplish the goal. Every time you complete an action, write a tally mark. Review your score every week, and study your progress. Are you making progress toward your goal? Is what you're doing getting you closer to your goal? If not, what needs to be changed in order to meet your goal? Cross off any actions that are not working and replace them with new ideas. Continue keeping score and adjusting your scoreboard until you have met your goal.

   a. What is your goal?

   _____

   _____

   _____

   _____

   _____

b. What actions do you need to take to accomplish
   your goal?

_____

_____

_____

_____

_____

_____

_____

_____

_____

_____

_____

_____

_____

_____

3. HELP SOMEONE. Think of one or more acts of
   kindness that you can do for others over the next
   two weeks. These could be as simple as helping
   your parents around the house or being a good
   friend. Use a scoreboard to write down the actions
   you took to complete your act(s) of kindness and

tally how many times you did them. At the end of each week, review your data. What do you notice? Was there an act that you did more than others? Would you do anything differently?

_____

_____

_____

_____

_____

_____

_____

_____

_____

_____

_____

_____

_____

_____

_____

_____

CHAPTER 7

FRIENDSHIP
Resolved: To Develop the Art and Science of Friendship

I know that everyone needs a true friend.

Big 6 Rules of Friendship:

1. True friends share interests.
2. True friends accept, approve, and appreciate one another, mistakes included.
3. True friends listen first.
4. True friends are proud of each other's accomplishments.
5. True friends are trustworthy.
6. True friends are loyal.

Did you know that the writer of *The Chronicles of Narnia* and the writer of *The Lord of the Rings* were best friends? In fact, even when J.R.R. Tolkien wanted to give up writing *The Lord of*

> "Friendship is the greatest of worldly goods. Certainly to me it is the chief happiness of life."
> —C. S. Lewis

the Rings, C. S. Lewis wouldn't let him. He saw just how amazing the story was going to be and encouraged his friend to keep working. It took Tolkien seventeen years to write that amazing story! Let's look at their friendship to see how they used the Big 6 Rules.

These two friends loved using their imaginations to tell stories to teach about the things they believed. They shared their stories and their progress with each other every Thursday night at their own club they created called the Inklings.

Tolkien and Lewis loved each other. Although they saw each other's weaknesses, each was careful about how he helped the other get better.

A friend is someone who knows you as you are,
understands where you have been, accepts who
you have become, and still invites you to grow.
—Unknown

People have two ears and one mouth. We should listen more than we speak. Tolkien was so unsure about his writing that he was often critical about his own stories. Lewis would listen carefully and gently reassure his friend of his abilities and the greatness of his work.

J.R.R. Tolkien

C.S. Lewis

Seeking first to understand, Lewis could clearly communicate his own feelings and understanding to help his friend.

True friends celebrate victories together. True friends should be each other's greatest cheerleaders. And true friends don't let jealousy ruin their friendship. As we will see in the chapter on conflict resolution, following this rule was a weakness in Lewis and Tolkien's relationship.

True friends stick to each other when times are easy—and even more so when times get tough. Several of Lewis and Tolkien's colleagues made fun of Tolkien's hobbits. It hurt him deeply. Lewis would often come to his friend's defense, praising his friend for his great work.

True friends are loyal. They speak positively and carefully of their friends, regardless of the situation. Lewis and Tolkien defended each other's character, honor, and reputation.

Perhaps neither *The Lord of the Rings* nor *The Chronicles of Narnia* would have been nearly so acclaimed if Lewis and Tolkien hadn't been true friends. Millions have enjoyed their stories thanks to this amazing friendship. The movies based on their novels are pretty cool too.

> **"The world is indeed full of peril, and in it there are many dark places; but still there is much that is fair, and though in all lands love is now mingled with grief, it grows perhaps the greater."**
> **—J.R.R. Tolkien**

WORKSHOP CHALLENGE

Talk About It

1. What are the Big 6 Rules of Friendship?

_____

_____

_____

_____

2. How do you think living the Big 6 Rules of Friendship influenced Lewis and Tolkien's friendship?

_____

_____

_____

_____

3. How would living the Big 6 Rules make a difference in your friendships?

_____

_____

_____

_____

4. When do you feel that you have lived one of the rules listed in the Big 6 with a friend? What happened? How did it make you feel?

_____

_____

_____

_____

_____

Go and Do

1. MAKE A LIST. Which of the rules in the Big 6 could you be better at? List which you could improve on and how you plan to do so.

_____

_____

_____

_____

_____

2. CREATE! Make three goals for improving your friendships, and track your progress over the next twenty-one days.

_____

_____

_____

_____

_____

_____

_____

_____

_____

_____

_____

_____

_____

_____

3. HELP SOMEONE. Can you improve a friendship?
   Share the Big 6 with a friend, and explain what
   they mean. Invite your friend to share with
   someone else. If you feel brave enough, and he
   or she is a good Rule 5 friend, share your goals
   with your friend, and ask him or her to help you
   accomplish your goals. Record your experience.

_____

_____

_____

_____

_____

_____

_____

CHAPTER 8

FINANCE
Resolved: To Develop Financial Intelligence

I know that wealth is built over time when my income is higher than my expenses.

No one knew in the growing port town of Boston way back on a cold winter day in January of 1706 that the new little baby Benjamin Franklin would become known as "The First Great American." Not many people throughout history can match his achievements in business, science, politics, and diplomacy. He helped build this nation with his fellow Founding Fathers! His efforts in politics and diplomacy are so impressive that his incredible achievements in business are often overlooked.

His brother was such a bully to him that, at the age of sixteen, he left his home and moved to Philadelphia. He worked as an apprentice to a printer but soon realized

he wouldn't achieve all the things he wanted if he didn't have money or was stuck working for someone else all day. Benjamin worked and saved until he could buy his own printing business. Even then, this did not satisfy him, and so he began purchasing other print shops and training workers to run them. As a result, he became the owner of several businesses that other people operated for him. Even more remarkable, he ended up owning eight of the fifteen newspapers printed in the early colonies.

Thanks to his understanding of finances, Benjamin Franklin was able to free himself from working on things for his survival so he could work on things that made him happy and helped others. He understood that money was a tool to free up his time for life. He spent money to make time, while others spent time to make money. He wrote, "Money never made a man happy yet, nor will it."

> **"An investment in knowledge always pays the best interest."**
> **—Often attributed to Benjamin Franklin**

Here are five simple rules of finance to consider:

1. Know how much you make, even if it's only a little. Keep track. Write it down in a notebook. If you don't know how much you make, you can't know how much you lose.
2. Know how much you spend. In the same notebook, keep track of every penny you spend. If

you subtract how much you spend from what you make, then you can know what your profits are.

3. Set a financial goal. The first goal you can make is to always spend less than what you make. Wealth is what you keep, not what you spend.

4. Never finance anything that depreciates. This simply means don't borrow money for something that is worth less the minute after you buy it.

5. Set a price limit. If what you are thinking about buying costs less than your price limit, then go ahead and buy it today. But if it costs more than the limit, then you should sleep on it for a night. If it's still that important to you the next day, then make a list of pros and cons to help you decide if it's worth it. If you have to work very hard to talk yourself into buying the item, it may not be worth it.

> "Your net worth to the world is usually determined by what remains after your bad habits are subtracted from your good ones."
> —Benjamin Franklin

> "Beware of little Expenses; a small Leak will sink a great Ship."
> —Benjamin Franklin

This is a list of some of Benjamin Franklin's incredible contributions:

1. He set up the world's first franchise-type model, freeing himself from the day-to-day work routine.
2. He invented the famed Franklin stove, improving heat efficiency of wood fires.
3. He created America's first volunteer fire department.
4. He founded an academy of learning in Philadelphia, which later became the University of Pennsylvania.
5. He founded America's first public library.
6. He discovered the relationship between lightning and electricity.
7. He invented the bifocal lens.
8. He was the first man to chart and study the temperatures of the Gulf Stream.
9. He published the bestselling *Poor Richard's Almanack* yearly.
10. He wrote one of the bestselling autobiographies of all time.
11. He revolutionized the mail service as Postmaster General.
12. He played an active part in the creation of nearly every major American document, including the Declaration of Independence, the  Constitution, the war alliance with France, and the peace treaty with England.

WORKSHOP CHALLENGE

Talk About It

1. What did Benjamin Franklin teach about money and happiness? Why do you think he said that?

_____

_____

_____

_____

_____

2. What do you think it means that he spent money to make time, while others spent time to make money?

_____

_____

_____

_____

_____

3. What difference do you think it might make if you start practicing these financial rules now?

_____

_____

_____

_____

_____

4. Have you already practiced one of the rules? What
   happened?

_____

_____

_____

_____

_____

_____

Go and Do

1. MAKE A LIST. Start keeping track of how much
   money you make, and keep track of all the money
   you spend. Be detailed.

   Income / From What?   Money Spent / On What?

2. CREATE! Set a goal to save. Remember to reward yourself, but don't spend all the money you save on your reward. Record your goal here.

_____

_____

_____

_____

_____

3. HELP SOMEONE. One of the great rewards of having control of your finances is your freedom to help others. Set a goal to help another regularly, even if it's only a small amount. Do it, and then record your experience.

_____

_____

_____

_____

_____

_____

_____

_____

CHAPTER 9

LEADERSHIP
Resolved: To Develop the Art and Science of Leadership

I know that everything rises and falls based on the leadership culture created in my community.

What is the difference between being a boss and being a leader? Are they the same thing? If you asked Sam Walton, founder of Walmart, he would probably tell you that being a boss and being a leader are very different.

Sam Walton was not born the billionaire business-man we now know him to be. However, eventually, he would grow a single discount store into a national chain of over 4,000 stores.

One of the secrets to his success was his ability to create a culture of leadership throughout his entire company. First and foremost, he knew that if he wanted strong leaders in his company, he would have to lead by example. Walton took responsibility for his actions, even when he made mistakes. He refused to "pass

> "We're all working together; that's the secret."
> —Sam Walton

the buck" (pass responsibility to someone else for his own actions). And he refused to be a victim, even when it would have been easier to do so.

Walton was a humble man, and his employees appreciated this quality in him. He was not threatened by other people in the company who wanted to be leaders just like he was. Nor was he afraid of people who were better than he was. In fact, he was always looking for great people who could share their unique talents for the benefit of his company and customers. Many times, he visited his competitors to see what they were doing better than he was and then used what he learned to improve his own stores. He was even on the lookout for talented people from these stores so that he could invite them to join his team.

> **"From this day forward, I solemnly promise and declare that every time a customer comes within ten feet of me, I will smile, look him in the eye, and greet him."**
> **—Sam Walton**

Once people joined the Walmart team, they were encouraged to work with others in a unified team. He expected his employees to help and support one another whenever they could. By doing this, his employees were able to share new ideas and lessons and spread these ideas across the company.

Walton also chose to live by the Golden Rule: "Do unto others as you would have them do unto you." He believed that treating his employees well (showing respect, encouraging talent, giving bonuses, and so on) would encourage them to choose to treat the customers well. And they did.

On April 5, 1992, Sam Walton passed away. Although he is gone, his legacy lives on. Wal-Mart Stores, Inc. continues to grow, and the employees and customers continue to benefit from the leadership culture that Walton established over sixty years ago.

WORKSHOP CHALLENGE

Talk About It

1. What leadership qualities did Sam Walton demonstrate?

_____

_____

_____

_____

_____

_____

2. How do you think Walmart became so successful?

_____

_____

_____

_____

_____

_____

3. Why do you think Walton wasn't afraid to hire people he thought were better than he was?

_____

_____

_____

_____

4. What does it mean to live by the Golden Rule? How did living by the Golden Rule help Sam Walton's business?

_____

_____

_____

_____

_____

_____

5. When have you lived the Golden Rule, and what difference did it make?

_____

_____

_____

_____

_____

6. What leadership qualities do you see in yourself?

_____

_____

_____

_____

_____

Go and Do

1. MAKE A LIST. Write down the qualities you believe
   a leader should demonstrate. Highlight the ones
   you have.

_____

_____

_____

_____

_____

_____

_____

2. CREATE! Write a letter to someone you admire
   (a relative, friend, business person, teacher, etc.)
   sharing the leadership qualities you see in that
   person and why you respect him or her. Record your
   experience after you receive a response to your letter.

_____

_____

_____

_____

_____

_____

_____

_____

3. HELP SOMEONE. How can you use your best leadership qualities to help others? Choose a quality, and write down one thing you can do with that quality to help someone by the end of the week. Now go and do it! Record your experience.

_____

_____

_____

_____

_____

_____

CHAPTER 10

CONFLICT RESOLUTION
Resolved: To Develop the Art and Science of Conflict Resolution

I know that being able to resolve conflict is essential to happiness, unity, and growth.

Remember our story from the chapter on friendship about J.R.R. Tolkien and C. S. Lewis? Remember how they helped each other be better because they were true friends? Well, the next chapter in their lives has a sad ending.

Only three years before Tolkien finished *The Lord of the Rings,* the two friends' lives started to take separate paths. Lewis enjoyed much fame and success from his writings, especially *The Chronicles of Narnia*, while Tolkien got very little. Lewis enjoyed popularity and new friendships and even got married, while Tolkien kept more and more to himself. Soon there were hurt feelings and misunderstandings that were never resolved. In fact, they never spoke again for the rest of their lives. It was a tragedy that could have been avoided.

There are some very simple tools these two amazing men could have used to fix their problem. First, identifying some of their mistakes might have been helpful. Sometimes when we get our feelings hurt, we decide to just get quiet. We sit there, upset, hurt, and bitter, but we don't ever say anything. On the other hand, we may get so angry that we become violent and try to hurt the person who hurt us. People can attack others physically or through gossip (the more cowardly way). Trying to hurt others' reputations or character is as bad as trying to hurt them physically.

Neither silence nor violence works. These just cause more hurt and anger until we become so obsessed that it interferes with our lives and disrupts other relationships.

So what can we do? What would have saved the relationship of two of the bestselling authors of all time? Five simple steps:

1. Affirm the relationship.
2. Seek to understand.
3. Seek to be understood.
4. Own responsibility by apologizing.
5. Seek agreement.

The first step simply means that the friendship is more important than the problem. It might be uncomfortable to face each other, but keeping that friend means more than holding on to that anger or hurt.

> "Friendship is... the sort of love one can imagine between angels."
> —C. S. Lewis

The second step is about the other person. We can't really resolve a problem if we don't understand the problem.

72

As some people say, "No matter how thin you slice the cheese, there are still two sides." We have to be able to step back and see both sides of the situation, when possible, or we will never really be able to fix the problem.

The third step is to seek to be understood. The goal isn't to blast the other person but just to address the issue. This requires honesty about the part we played and a willingness to give the other person the benefit of the doubt. If we focus on the problem and not the person, we are more likely to fix the problem.

The fourth step is to own as much of the conflict as possible while still being truthful. For some reason, many people see apologizing as a show of guilt or fault or even weakness. But apologizing opens the door to forgiveness and makes resolution possible. The problem is that we usually don't see that we are part of the problem.

> **"It is not the strength of the body that counts, but the strength of the spirit."**
> **—Often attributed to J.R.R. Tolkien**

The fifth and final step is to seek agreement. Agreeing to work together from this point forward creates unity and strength for the future. We have understood each other, apologized as needed, and are ready to work together from now on.

What might have happened if these two favorite writers had slowed down enough to follow these steps together? What else could they have possibly accomplished, even if it was only to have peace in their lives? Unfortunately C. S. Lewis passed away before they could ever make it right.

Let's resolve together to remember that our relationships are more important than our problems.

WORKSHOP CHALLENGE

Talk About It

1. From what you read, what do you think could be some reasons why J.R.R. Tolkien and C. S. Lewis had a conflict?

   _____

   _____

   _____

   _____

   _____

2. How could they have fixed the problem?

   _____

   _____

   _____

   _____

   _____

   _____

3. Why is being able to resolve problems with family and friends so important?

_____

_____

_____

_____

_____

_____

4. Can you identify a relationship where you could use the five steps to resolve a problem?

_____

_____

_____

_____

_____

_____

5. What difference would it make if you practiced these steps in your relationships?

_____

_____

_____

_____

_____

_____

6. When have you successfully resolved a conflict with a friend or family member? How did it feel?

_____

_____

_____

_____

_____

Go and Do

1. MAKE A LIST. Write about a time when you had your feelings hurt. Were you able to resolve it? What did you need to do to make it right? Is there someone that you have offended? What do you need to do to make it right?

_____

_____

_____

_____

_____

2. CREATE! Write a goal for improving your conflict resolution skills. What can you do to enhance your ability to resolve problems with your friends and family?

_____

_____

_____

_____

3. HELP SOMEONE. Do you know someone who needs help with this? Could this help a person who is being bullied? Or could it help the bully? Identify someone you sense could use this, and share what you have learned with that person. Record your experience.

_____

_____

_____

_____

_____

_____

_____

_____

CHAPTER 11

SYSTEMS
Resolved: To Develop
Systems Thinking

*I know that by seeing life as connected patterns,
I improve my opportunity to succeed and
help many people.*

Systems are everywhere. Just think about the kinds of systems it takes to fill one glass of water. We need a glass that we bought from a store and that others made in their factory. We need the faucet and the plumbing, the water transportation services, and the water storage and purification plants, and that's just to name a few. It's amazing what must be done just to get a simple glass of water!

McDonald's is a perfect example of an excellent system. The McDonald brothers started with a single little restaurant. They had all kinds of foods on their menu, and they had to work very

> "If you work just for money, you'll never make it, but if you love what you're doing and you always put the customer first, success will be yours."
> —Ray Kroc

hard to prepare all the different foods. Then one day, they realized that what people bought most were their hamburgers.

They developed the first ever assembly line for hamburgers. They could serve hundreds of hamburgers, and they could hire anyone to cook rather than a specialized chef because of how simple their system was. They built their own school for teaching people how to run their stores called Hamburger University.

They learned that having well-defined processes—for everything from how to build the building to which colors to use, how to balance the budget, how much food and supplies to buy and when, and how to build a good hamburger—made the job of every owner of a McDonald's store very simple. They learned that if they let their workers suggest ideas for improvement, they could be even more efficient and successful. This is how they got the ideas for Big Macs, Egg McMuffins, and Filet-O-Fish sandwiches!

The McDonald brothers sold their system to Ray Kroc, who discovered that as he planned carefully, tried the plan, checked to see how it worked, and adjusted to make it better, he could quickly grow the business and sell a whole lot of hamburgers all over the world.

> **"Luck is a dividend of sweat. The more you sweat, the luckier you get."**
> **—Ray Kroc**

These lessons taught that little adjustments would have a powerful effect for people everywhere.

When we develop effective systems and allow people to use their imaginations within those systems, our potential is limitless.

WORKSHOP CHALLENGE

Talk About It

1. What was the McDonald brothers' great invention?

_____

_____

_____

_____

_____

_____

2. How has their invention changed the world?

_____

_____

_____

_____

_____

_____

3. What lessons did they learn about systems and people?

_____

_____

_____

_____

_____

_____

4. Can you identify and explain a system you are familiar with?

_____

_____

_____

_____

_____

_____

5. What difference would it make if you started to see the systems in everything?

_____

_____

_____

_____

_____

6. When have you noticed or even created a system, and what were the results?

_____

_____

_____

_____

_____

Go and Do

1. MAKE A LIST. Start noticing systems. Try to observe at least one system each day, and write down as many parts to that system as you can think of. With your parents' permission, get on the Internet and research as much about that system as you can find. Do this for two weeks, recording your findings every day. What did you learn?

_____

_____

_____

_____

_____

_____

_____

2. CREATE! Develop your own system. It doesn't matter what it is for, but write it down, draw it out, and build it. Keep a record of what you were able to do.

_____

_____

_____

_____

_____

_____

3. HELP SOMEONE. Can you create a system that could help others? Can you help make another person's life easier because of something you create? Be sure to record everything. Remember, keeping a record and a scoreboard will not only help you keep on track, but it will inspire new ideas in the future as well.

_____

_____

_____

_____

_____

_____

_____

_____

CHAPTER 12

ADVERSITY QUOTIENT (AQ)
Resolved: To Develop Adversity Quotient

I know that AQ helps me overcome obstacles.

Adversity quotient (AQ)—that might sound like a difficult term to understand. But with a little explanation, you will not only get it but strive for it. AQ is our ability to endure challenges in life. We all have challenges—everyone. No one has a perfect, beautiful, easy, breezy life.

The way we see and handle our challenges will largely determine our success in life. Learning to strengthen our AQ then increases our potential for success in achieving our goals.

Billy Durant was the founder of the car company that built Buick, General Motors (GM), Chevrolet, and

Durant Motors. He started with nothing and ended with

nothing. But the "in-between" was amazing! Only a few years into building his first automotive giant, GM, he lost everything when the economy went bad. The bank took his company. He had nothing. This challenge would have made most men quit. Not Billy. He teamed up with a man named Louis Chevrolet, and within a few years, this new company, Chevrolet, was doing so well that Billy was able to buy GM back from the bank.

This occurred during the 1920s. He was one of only a handful of multimillionaires in the United States. He was so driven that he didn't notice some of his business partners were taking advantage of him. It wasn't long before he lost everything again. But he didn't give up. His ability to fight discouragement was astounding. He built yet another car company, Durant Motors. However, when the Great Depression hit in 1929, he lost everything for a third time.

> "If you continuously compete with others, you become bitter, but if you continuously compete with yourself, you become better."
> —Unknown

Even with these setbacks, he never gave up. He took them as a personal challenge to work even harder. It is sad, but many people give up when something challenging happens.

How did he do it? How could he get back up after encountering such obstacles and setbacks? The solution is simple. Zig Ziglar said, "The chief cause of failure and unhappiness is trading what you want most for what you want right now." Billy knew what he wanted, and nothing—no hardship, no trial, no challenge—would lessen his faith in his purpose and accomplishing his goals.

> **"Forget past mistakes. Forget failures. Forget everything except what you are going to do now and do it."**
> **—Billy Durant**

WORKSHOP CHALLENGE

Talk About It

1. Do your best to describe what adversity quotient (AQ) is.

_____

_____

_____

_____

_____

_____

_____

_____

_____

2. How did Billy Durant show his AQ?

_____

_____

_____

_____

_____

_____

3. Why is increasing our AQ so important?

_____

_____

_____

_____

_____

_____

_____

4. Who do you know that has a high AQ? Share how
   you know this.

_____

_____

_____

_____

_____

_____

Go and Do

1. MAKE A LIST. List some of the most difficult challenges you have faced. How did you get through them? What lessons did you learn? How can what you learned help you with future challenges?

_____

_____

_____

_____

_____

_____

_____

_____

2. CREATE! Make a plan for how you are going to manage future challenges in your life. What questions could you ask yourself during a challenging situation that might help you work through it?

_____

_____

_____

_____

_____

_____

_____

3. HELP SOMEONE. Teach a friend or family member about AQ. Invite him or her to describe a difficult, challenging experience he or she has been through and how not giving up helped. Record your experience.

_____

_____

_____

_____

_____

_____

_____

CHAPTER 13

LEGACY
Resolved: To Keep Moving Forward in My Field of Mastery

I know that a true legacy leaves the world a
better place than I found it.

A legacy is something left to our children or to our country, community, school, etc. It could be money, service, or a great example to follow of character, courage, or overcoming pain or tragedy. As you read about what our forefathers accomplished, think about the incredible legacy they left so we could be free to create our own.

> "Freedom is not a gift bestowed upon us by other men, but a right that belongs to us by the laws of God and nature."
> —Often attributed to Benjamin Franklin

John Adams, Benjamin Franklin, Alexander Hamilton, John Jay, Thomas Jefferson, James Madison, George Washington, and many others—more than 200 years ago, this group of men, known today as the Founding Fathers, gathered in Philadelphia, Pennsylvania, to set in motion what would become their greatest legacy. Together they would craft the Declaration of Independence and the United States Constitution to ensure the future of the United States of America and reverse the decline of the New England colonies.

It began in the late 1600s, when the colonies were unable to pay their soldiers following a failed expedition to the French colony of Quebec. The discontented soldiers returned to Boston, Massachusetts, where they demanded payment for their service. The government's attempt to raise funds to pay the soldiers failed. They began to worry that the more upset the soldiers became, the more likely they would be to use their weapons against government officials and citizens of Boston. So the government came up with the idea of printing £7,000 of paper notes. Unfortunately, they did so without backing the notes with gold or any other valuable item, thus making the notes valueless. This is known as fiat money or Continental currency. It was decided that this fiat money would be used to pay the soldiers' salaries.

The government knew there was a chance the public would not accept the paper notes, so they tried to ease their fears by making two promises. First, they promised that over the next two years, the paper notes would be backed by gold and silver from tax revenues. Second, they promised to never print paper notes again. It took only four months before the government broke both promises. Their simple, short-term solution for paying the soldiers quickly turned into a disaster. Printing fiat money was the government's idea of an easy fix. Any time a problem arose which required funding, they just printed more. To them, this was much easier than actually having to collect more in taxes or make plans to reduce spending.

By the mid-1700s, leading up to the Revolutionary War, millions of dollars in fiat money had been printed. The more they printed, the less it was valued. Citizens began to realize that the fiat money was fraudulent and worthless. Deeply in debt after winning the Revolutionary War, colonial America was finally bankrupted by the fiat money.

The Founding Fathers disapproved of the printing of fiat money, and at the Constitutional Convention, they looked for a way to bring the colonies out of their financial crisis. By this time, the colonies had learned the painful lesson of fiat money and unanimously voted to include in the United States Constitution a ban on ever printing it again. (Unfortunately, the Founding Fathers' admonition against fiat money was abandoned after America's Civil War.)

Through the creation of the Constitution, the Founding Fathers were able to reverse the decline of colonial America. They created an ethnically diverse community of citizens who valued the freedom to pursue one's dreams through character and work ethic without government interference. They were also anxious to protect America from another such decline.

"Those who would give up essential Liberty, to purchase a little temporary Safety, deserve neither Liberty nor Safety."
—Benjamin Franklin, in a letter from the Pennsylvania Assembly to the governor dated Nov. 11, 1755

The legacy of the Founding Fathers has been passed from generation to generation and continues to influence us today. It is now our turn to take on the responsibility of upholding their legacy so that it remains intact for all the generations following us. In addition, we are challenged with the opportunity to leave our own legacy to future generations, which will bless their lives.

WORKSHOP CHALLENGE

Talk About It

1. What does it mean to leave a legacy?

_____

_____

_____

_____

2. What events led up to the decline of colonial America?

_____

_____

_____

_____

_____

3. What are the disadvantages of short-term thinking?

_____

_____

_____

_____

_____

_____

4. Which historical documents helped reverse colonial America's decline?

_____

_____

_____

_____

_____

_____

5. What legacy did the Founding Fathers establish?

_____

_____

_____

_____

_____

_____

6. How does the Founding Fathers' legacy live on today?

_____

_____

_____

_____

_____

_____

_____

_____

_____

7. Do you know someone who has left a legacy? Describe that person and what he or she has accomplished.

_____

_____

_____

_____

_____

_____

_____

_____

_____

Go and Do

1. MAKE A LIST. Imagine yourself twenty years from now. What legacy do you want to leave to your school? Your family? Your community? Make a list of what you would like your friends, loved ones, and the community to remember about you. What will your legacy be?

   _____

   _____

   _____

   _____

   _____

   _____

2. CREATE! Think of a person from today or the past whose legacy you admire. Write a letter thanking this person for his or her contributions. Explain how his or her legacy has affected your life, and share what you will do to help that legacy continue into the future.

   _____

   _____

   _____

   _____

   _____

   _____

3. HELP SOMEONE. You can never be too young to leave a legacy. Think of something you can do to help the community (a winter coat collection, an after-school program, etc.). As you put together your plan of action, make a note of what you would like to accomplish and who you are trying to help. How can the work you do create a legacy? How will people be affected by your legacy?

_____

_____

_____

_____

_____

_____

_____

_____

_____

Acknowledgments

I would like to thank Orrin Woodward, Chris Brady, and the entire LIFE Leadership team for their faith, trust, and open hearts and minds. Thank you to my beautiful wife Lynette and my children Wyatt, Madison, Rylee, Hayden, and Tayt. Special thanks to my dad, Ed Brown, and Cristina Schubert for their amazing efforts to make this book a reality. And thanks to Chad and Julie Palmer and Rob and Kenyon Robson, who swung wide open the doors of LIFE Leadership and let me in.

Rob Brown

Subscriptions and Products from
LIFE Leadership

Rascal Radio Subscription
Rascal Radio by LIFE Leadership is the world's first online personal development radio hot spot. Rascal Radio is centered on LIFE Leadership's 8 Fs: Faith, Family, Finances, Fitness, Following, Freedom, Friends, and Fun. Subscribers have unlimited access to **hundreds and hundreds** of audio recordings that they can stream endlessly from both the **LIFE Leadership website** and the **LIFE Leadership Smartphone App.** Listen to one of the preset stations or customize your own based on speaker or subject. Of course, you can easily skip tracks or "like" as many as you want. And if you are listening from the website, you can purchase any one of these incredible audios.

Let Rascal Radio provide you with **life-changing information to help you live the life you've always wanted!**

Edge **by Chris Brady and Orrin Woodward**
There's no age limit on success or the thinking behind it. Get the *Edge* on insight, inspiration, and plenty of practical advice by studying the experience of those who have already gone through the learning curve and achieved the kind of victories and fulfillment you strive for. Challenge yourself playing "Find Obstaclés," that annoying elf-like creature who (like real-life critics) will do anything to trip you up on your road to

success. The life-changing information found in this book will help you develop a keen eye and the good sense to easily spot him and avoid his snares. No one else can be who you are or do what you do. All your dreams deserve your best efforts, so get *Edge* and get a head start on accomplishing them!

The Edge Series

You'll cut in front of the rest of the crowd when you get the *Edge*. Designed for those on the younger side of life, this hard-core, no-frills series promotes self-confidence, drive, and motivation. Get advice, timely information, and true stories of success from interesting talks and fascinating people. Block out the noise around you and learn the principles of self-improvement at an early age. It's a gift that will keep on giving throughout your life. Subscribe today and get a competitive *Edge* on tomorrow.

Series includes 1 audio monthly.

Financial Fitness for Teens: 6 Steps from Broke to Abundant from the LIFE Leadership Essentials Series with Foreword by Chris Brady

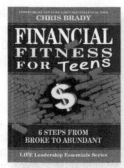

It's never too earlyto learn the principles of financial success. But schools often skip right over this crucial topic. And by the time many adults figure out that they don't know how to properly manage their money, they are often buried in debt and feeling helpless to dig themselves out. Financial Fitness for Teens aims to fill in the gap, break the cycle of bad financial habits and misinformation being passed down from generation to generation, and show you how easy and exciting financial fitness can be. "The money thing" is one of the most important aspects of life to master—and the sooner, the better!

FINANCIAL FITNESS PROGRAM

Get Out of Debt and Stay Out of Debt!

FREE PERSONAL WEBSITE
SIGN UP AND TAKE ADVANTAGE OF THESE FREE FEATURES:

- Personal website
- Take your custom assessment test
- Build your own profile
- Share milestones and successes with partners and friends
- Post videos and photos
- Receive daily info "nuggets"

FINANCIAL FITNESS BASIC PROGRAM

The first program to teach all three aspects of personal finance: defense, offense, and playing field. Learn the simple, easy-to-apply principles that can help you shore up your resources, get out of debt, and build stability for a more secure future. It's all here, including a comprehensive book, companion workbook, and 8 audios that amplify the teachings from the books.

Also available DIGITALLY!

FINANCIAL FITNESS MASTER CLASS

Buy it once and use it forever! Designed to provide a continual follow-up to the principles learned in the Basic Program, this ongoing educational support offers over 6 hours of video and over 14 hours of audio instruction that walk you through the workbook, step by step. Perfect for individual or group study.
6 videos, 15 audios

FINANCIAL FITNESS TRACK AND SAVE

The Financial Fitness Program teaches you how to get out of debt, build additional streams of income, and properly take advantage of tax deductions. Now, with this subscription, we give you the tools to do so. The Tracker offers mobile expense tracking tools and budgeting software, while the Saver offers you thousands of coupons and discounts to help you save money every day.